The Order of Things

Put the pictures in order so they r

Use Tiles 1, 2, and 3.

Use Tiles 4, 5, and 6.

Use Tiles 7, 8, and 9.

Use Tiles 10, 11, and 12.

Think about what you would do first, next, and last!

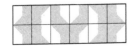

Objective: Determine the sequence of three pictured events.

1

The Things I Do

Put the sentences in order so they make sense.

In My Day
Use Tiles 1, 2, and 3.

A

I get dressed.

K

I wake up.

D

I go to school.

How I Play
Use Tiles 4, 5, and 6.

F

I get my towel and suit.

H

I swim in the pool.

J

I go to the pool.

Fishing Fun
Use Tiles 7, 8, and 9.

L

I get my rod.

C

I catch a fish.

G

I go to the lake.

Suppertime
Use Tiles 10, 11, and 12.

B

We eat dinner.

E

I set the table.

I

I call my family.

Objective: Determine the sequence of three descriptive events.

Order, Please!

Put the sentences in order so they make sense.

My Pen Pal   **Use Tiles 1, 2, and 3.**

> **E**
> Then, mail the letter.

> **D**
> First, write the letter.

> **B**
> Next, sign the letter.

A Helping Hand   **Use Tiles 4, 5, and 6.**

> **C**
> First, wash the clothes.

> **A**
> Then, fold the clothes.

> **K**
> Next, dry the clothes.

The words first, next, and then help you put things in order!

At Bedtime   **Use Tiles 7, 8, and 9.**

> **F**
> Then, go to sleep.

> **J**
> Take a bath.

> **H**
> Next, read a story.

A Hungry Cat   **Use Tiles 10, 11, and 12.**

> **I**
> Open the cat food.

> **L**
> Put the food in the dish.

> **G**
> Then, give the food to the cat.

Objective: Determine the sequence of three-step directions, using clue words.

3

Cooking Fun!

Put the sentences in order.

Pancakes for Breakfast   Use Tiles 1, 2, and 3.

E

Next, mix the batter.

A

First, break the eggs.

I

Cook the batter.

Juice for Us   Use Tiles 4, 5, and 6.

C

Cut the oranges in half.

B

Get three oranges.

F

Squeeze the oranges.

Tossed Salad   Use Tiles 7, 8, and 9.

D

Mix them in a bowl.

K

Cut the vegetables.

H

Buy the vegetables.

Apple Pie for Me   Use Tiles 10, 11, and 12.

G

Wash the apples.

L

Cut the apples.

J

Peel the apples.

Objective: Determine the sequence of three-step recipes.

Step by Step

Put the sentences in order.

Play with Friends
Use Tiles 1, 2, and 3.

H
Meet your friends at the park.

L
Call your friends.

C
Play a ball game.

Read for Fun
Use Tiles 4, 5, and 6.

G
Read the book.

K
Go to the library.

I
Check out a book.

Show Your Picture
Use Tiles 7, 8, and 9.

D
Hang your picture on the wall.

F
Get some paper and paints.

A
Paint a pretty picture.

Give a Gift
Use Tiles 10, 11, and 12.

B
Wrap the box with pretty paper.

J
Put the gift in a box.

E
Get a gift at the store.

Objective: Determine the sequence of three-step directions.

5

Letters in Order

Answer (Yes ☺) or (No ☹) .

The letters of the alphabet are always in the same order.

a b c d e f g h i j k l m n o p q r s t u v w x y z

1 Does c come before d? J (Yes ☺) H (No ☹)

2 Does t come before s? L (Yes ☺) K (No ☹)

3 Does m come before n? H (Yes ☺) C (No ☹)

4 Does j come after i? I (Yes ☺) A (No ☹)

5 Does h come after g? A (Yes ☺) E (No ☹)

6 Does b come after c? F (Yes ☺) J (No ☹)

7 Does d come before e? C (Yes ☺) B (No ☹)

8 Does w come before v? E (Yes ☺) F (No ☹)

9 Does f come before e? D (Yes ☺) G (No ☹)

10 Does k come after l? K (Yes ☺) D (No ☹)

11 Does i come after h? B (Yes ☺) I (No ☹)

12 Does d come before c? G (Yes ☺) E (No ☹)

Objective: Identify letters that come before or after other letters in the alphabet.

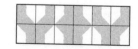

Letters in Place

Answer Yes 😊 or No ☹ .

Look carefully for clue words like **before**, **after**, **first**, and **last**.

a b c d e f g h i j k l m n o p q r s t u v w x y z

1. Does **j** come before **l**?   L [Yes 😊]   J [No ☹]

2. Does **t** come after **u**?   C [Yes 😊]   D [No ☹]

3. Does **n** come before **o**?   G [Yes 😊]   A [No ☹]

4. Does **p** come after **q**?   D [Yes 😊]   K [No ☹]

5. Is **b** the second letter?   A [Yes 😊]   F [No ☹]

6. Is **y** the last letter?   E [Yes 😊]   C [No ☹]

7. Is **d** the fifth letter?   B [Yes 😊]   E [No ☹]

8. Does **g** come before **h**?   J [Yes 😊]   G [No ☹]

9. Does **n** come after **m**?   H [Yes 😊]   I [No ☹]

10. Is **c** two places after **a**?   F [Yes 😊]   L [No ☹]

11. Does **s** come after **t**?   K [Yes 😊]   B [No ☹]

12. Does **r** come before **s**?   I [Yes 😊]   H [No ☹]

Letters Before and After

Find each letter. Follow the clues.

a b c d e f g h i j k l m n o p q r s t u v w x y z

Clues

1 the letter after **a**

2 the letter before **n**

3 the last letter

4 the first letter

5 the letter before **e**

6 the letter after **p**

7 the letter after **h**

8 the letter before **k**

9 the letter before **m**

10 the third letter

11 the fifth letter

12 the letter before **z**

Answer Box

A	B	C	D	E	F
m	q	c	a	l	z
G	**H**	**I**	**J**	**K**	**L**
j	y	b	i	e	d

Objective: Identify the position of individual letters in the alphabet.

Letter Groups

Find the missing letter.

a b c d e f g h i j k l m n o p q r s t u v w x y z

1. a b ▪

2. x y ▪

3. ▪ x y

4. ▪ u v

5. e f ▪

6. l m ▪

7. q ▪ s

8. d ▪ f

9. j ▪ l

10. ▪ b c

11. t u ▪

12. ▪ y z

Sing the Alphabet Song. The letters are in groups. Learn the letters for each group.

Answer Box

A	B	C	D	E	F
t	c	v	g	n	z

G	H	I	J	K	L
r	a	w	k	x	e

Objective: Identify the letter that completes an alphabetical grouping.

All around the Alphabet

Choose the letter that comes first in ABC order.

a b c d e f g h i j k l m n o p q r s t u v w x y z

1. f   e   g
2. b   a   c
3. c   d   b
4. e   f   d
5. i   j   h
6. g   h   f
7. u   t   v
8. o   n   p
9. w   x   y
10. p   q   o
11. w   x   v
12. s   r   t

Look at the letters p, b, and g. Which letter comes first in ABC order?

Answer Box

A	B	C	D	E	F
w	b	a	f	e	d

G	H	I	J	K	L
h	v	r	n	t	o

Objective: Identify the letter in a set that comes first in the alphabet.

ABC Order

Answer or .

The word <u>d</u>og begins with <u>d</u>.
The word <u>r</u>ug begins with <u>r</u>.
Which word comes first?

a b c d e f g h i j k l m n o p q r s t u v w x y z
      ↓   ↓
  dog   **rug**

1. Does **h**at come before **c**oat?   D Yes 😊   L No ☹

2. Does **l**ake come before **s**ea?   H Yes 😊   F No ☹

3. Does **m**an come before **t**urtle?   I Yes 😊   G No ☹

4. Does **y**ou come before **m**e?   A Yes 😊   K No ☹

5. Does **s**it come before **r**un?   J Yes 😊   D No ☹

6. Does **b**all come before **c**ar?   G Yes 😊   I No ☹

7. Does **o**ne come before **t**wo?   F Yes 😊   H No ☹

8. Does **b**at come before **a**nt?   L Yes 😊   A No ☹

9. Does **p**an come before **n**ap?   B Yes 😊   J No ☹

10. Does **s**un come before **t**ug?   E Yes 😊   C No ☹

11. Does **h**ope come before **m**op?   C Yes 😊   E No ☹

12. Does **h**ill come before **f**ill?   K Yes 😊   B No ☹

Objective: Put word pairs in alphabetical order.

Word Groups

Tell if each set of words is in ABC order.

Look at the beginning letter in each word. Which letter comes first in ABC order?

a b c d e f g h i j k l m n o p q r s t u v w x y z

     ↓   ↓   ↓

  girl   **kite**   **pan**

#							
1	apple	bike	hat	J	Yes 😊	A	No ☹
2	egg	bug	doll	C	Yes 😊	L	No ☹
3	ball	cat	fish	A	Yes 😊	D	No ☹
4	tiger	zebra	monkey	F	Yes 😊	C	No ☹
5	park	shop	zoo	G	Yes 😊	B	No ☹
6	car	boat	ship	H	Yes 😊	E	No ☹
7	baby	girl	woman	I	Yes 😊	G	No ☹
8	rice	carrots	beets	L	Yes 😊	F	No ☹
9	grass	flower	tree	E	Yes 😊	H	No ☹
10	me	we	you	D	Yes 😊	K	No ☹
11	box	gift	party	B	Yes 😊	I	No ☹
12	cow	pig	sheep	K	Yes 😊	J	No ☹

Objective: Put word groups in alphabetical order.

What Is in a Word Book?

Find the words that belong under each heading.

A Word Book has words and pictures. The words are in ABC order.

Animals	People	Places	Things
1	4	7	10
2	5	8	11
3	6	9	12

Answer Box

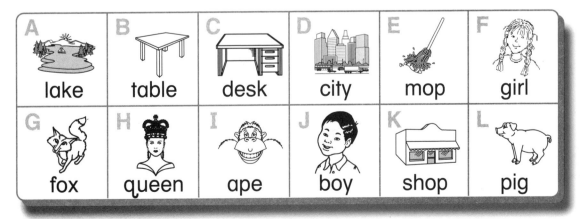

A lake	B table	C desk	D city	E mop	F girl
G fox	H queen	I ape	J boy	K shop	L pig

A Word Book Page

Look at the Word Book page. Read the word that names each picture.

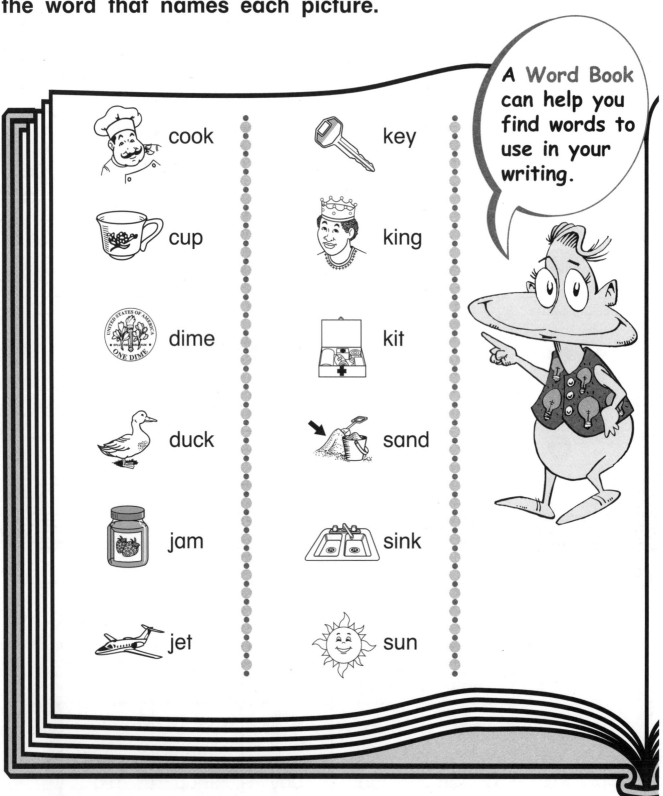

A Word Book can help you find words to use in your writing.

cook

cup

dime

duck

jam

jet

key

king

kit

sand

sink

sun

Objective: Recognize the purpose of a Word Book.

Now finish each sentence. Find a word from the Word Book.

1 The ■ is hot at noon.   **Find an s word.**

2 The ■ will make food.   **Find a c word.**

3 He drinks milk from a ■.   **Find a c word.**

4 She puts ■ on the bread.   **Find a j word.**

5 This pencil costs one ■.   **Find a d word.**

6 Use a ■ to open the door.   **Find a k word.**

7 The dish is in the ■.   **Find an s word.**

8 Get some tape from the ■.   **Find a k word.**

9 I put ■ in my pail.   **Find an s word.**

10 A ■ can fly high in the sky.   **Find a j word.**

11 Look at the ■ with a crown!   **Find a k word.**

12 A ■ swims in the pond.   **Find a d word.**

Answer Box

A	B	C	D	E	F
key	cook	jam	sun	cup	sand

G	H	I	J	K	L
kit	duck	jet	sink	king	dime

Objective: Find entries in a Word Book, using picture clues and context.

What Is in a Book?

Read the Contents page in a science book.

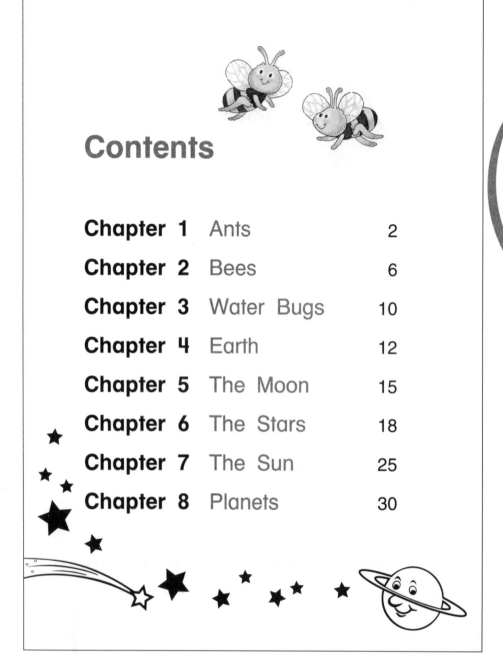

Contents

The Contents page tells what is in a book. It also tells where to find something in the book.

**Now finish each sentence about the science book.
Use the Contents page to help you.**

1. The book has  chapters.

2. Chapter 1 tells about ▪.

3. Chapter 2 begins on ▪.

4. Chapter 2 tells about ▪.

5. Chapter 3 begins on ▪.

6. Chapter 3 tells about ▪.

7. Chapter 4 begins on ▪.

8. Chapter 4 tells about ▪.

9. Chapter 5 begins on ▪.

10. Chapter 6 tells about ▪.

11. Learn about the sun in ▪.

12. Learn about planets in ▪.

> The chapter name is a clue to what is in the chapter.

Answer Box

A	B	C	D	E	F
page 12	the stars	water bugs	Earth	page 10	Chapter 7
G	**H**	**I**	**J**	**K**	**L**
bees	eight	Chapter 8	ants	page 6	page 15

Objective: Find information in a table of contents.

What Is in a Chapter?

Read the Contents page.

Contents

Finish each sentence about the Contents page.

1 The book has ■ chapters.

2 Chapter 1 tells about ■.

3 Chapter 3 tells about ■.

4 Chapter 2 begins on ■.

5 Chapter 4 tells about ■.

6 Chapter 6 begins on ■.

Now find the chapter that has the answer to each question.

7 Do bears eat fish?

8 Which bear is all white?

9 How big are bear cubs?

10 Do bears sleep in winter?

11 Do bears run fast?

12 Do bears live in caves?

Think. Each question has clue words to help you find the chapter.

Answer Box

A	B	C	D	E	F
six	Chapter 3	Chapter 5	How Bears Run	Kinds of Bears	Chapter 2
G	**H**	**I**	**J**	**K**	**L**
Chapter 6	page 11	Chapter 4	What Bears Eat	Chapter 1	page 30

Objective: Make inferences about information in a book, using a table of contents.

19

Parts of a Book

A book has names for all its parts. Look at the parts. Think about what each part tells you.

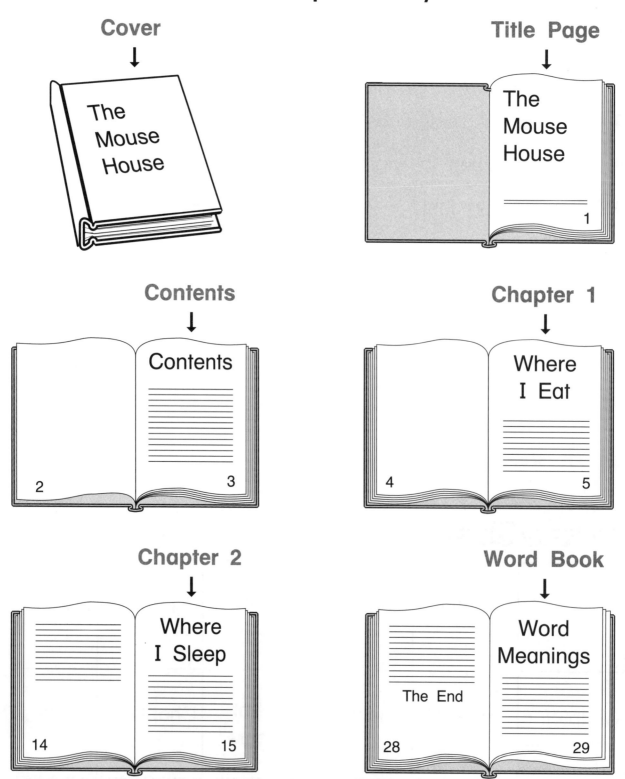

Cover → The Mouse House

Title Page → The Mouse House · 1

Contents → Contents · 2 · 3

Chapter 1 → Where I Eat · 4 · 5

Chapter 2 → Where I Sleep · 14 · 15

Word Book → Word Meanings · The End · 28 · 29

Objective: Recognize parts of a book.

Now finish each sentence about the book.

1. The outside of a book is called a ▪.

2. The Title Page tells about ▪.

3. The Word Book is at the ▪.

4. The Title Page is at the ▪.

5. Chapter 1 tells about ▪.

6. Chapter 1 begins on page ▪.

7. Chapter 1 ends on page ▪.

8. The Title Page is on page ▪.

9. The Contents is on page ▪.

10. Chapter 2 begins on page ▪.

11. The story ends on page ▪.

12. The word meanings start on page ▪.

Each part of a book tells something different. Knowing about each part helps you use the book.

Answer Box

A	B	C	D	E	F
end	3	5	the name of the book	beginning	cover
G	**H**	**I**	**J**	**K**	**L**
where the mouse eats	28	29	1	14	15

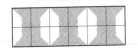

Objective: Find information in parts of a book, using a diagram with callouts.

21

All about Me

Finish each sentence. Use the picture to help you.

1. The boy sees with his ■.

2. He hears with his ■.

3. He smells with his ■.

4. He smiles with his ■.

5. Dark ■ grows on his head.

6. His head is on his ■.

7. He hugs his mom with his ■.

8. He holds things with his ■.

9. His heart is in his ■.

10. He walks on his two ■.

11. He likes to play in his bare ■.

12. He wiggles his ten ■.

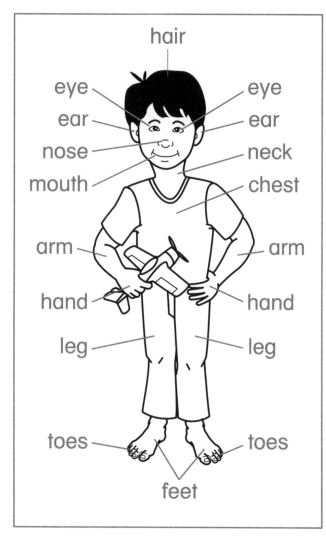

Answer Box

A	B	C	D	E	F
nose	chest	toes	hands	mouth	eyes

G	H	I	J	K	L
hair	feet	neck	ears	arms	legs

Objective: Identify parts of the body, using a diagram and context clues.

All about My Pets

Finish each sentence about the pets.
Use the pictures to help you.

1. The bird has a tail made of ▪.

2. The bird flies with its ▪.

3. The bird eats with its ▪.

4. The bird sees with its ▪.

5. The dog has four ▪.

6. The dog wags its ▪.

7. The dog smells with its ▪.

8. The dog barks with its ▪.

9. The cat stands on its ▪.

10. The cat bites with its ▪.

11. The cat scratches with its ▪.

12. The cat has a coat made of ▪.

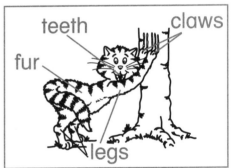

 **Answer Box** ···

A	B	C	D	E	F
beak	claws	nose	teeth	fur	wings
G	H	I	J	K	L
paws	legs	eyes	feathers	tail	mouth

Objective: Identify parts of a bird, a dog, and a cat, using a diagram and context clues.

23

Around the Classroom

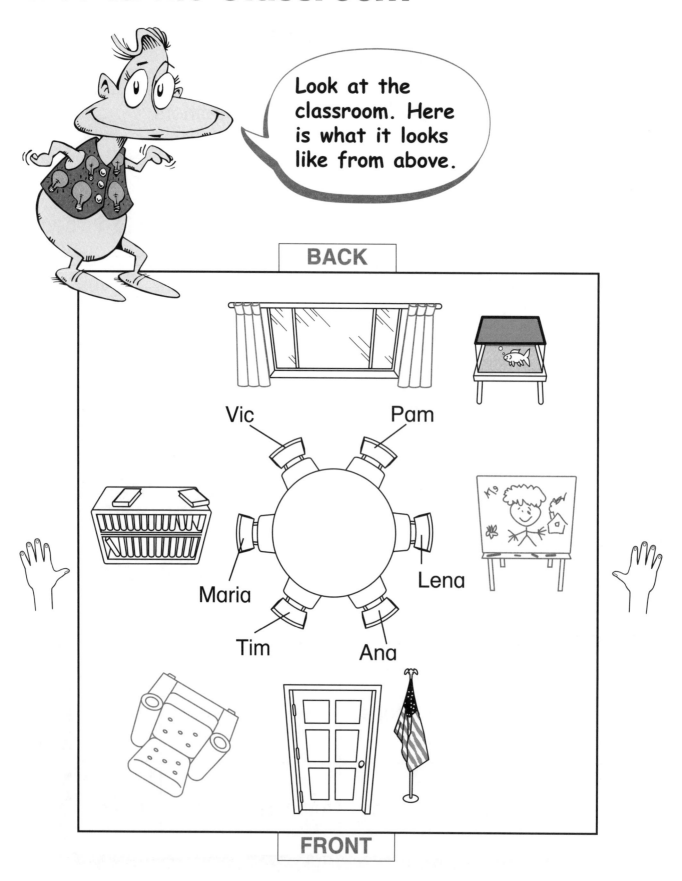

Objective: Interpret a diagram of an area viewed from above.

Finish each sentence about the classroom. Use the words front, back, right, and left.

① The door is at the ▪.

② The window is at the ▪.

③ The bookcase is at the ▪.

④ The art center is at the ▪.

Now finish each of these sentences.

⑤ The flag is beside the ▪.

⑥ The bookcase is behind the ▪.

⑦ The fish tank is beside the ▪.

⑧ The ▪ is in the middle of the room.

⑨ The fish tank is behind the ▪.

⑩ Maria sits between ▪.

⑪ Pam sits between ▪.

⑫ Ana sits between ▪.

Look for clue words like beside and behind. Think about their meaning.

Answer Box

A	B	C	D	E	F
Tim and Lena	round table	left	art center	window	Vic and Tim

G	H	I	J	K	L
back	big chair	door	Vic and Lena	front	right

May We Vote?

Read each chart.

Votes for New School Hours

7:00 to 1:00	✔	✔	✔	✔		
8:00 to 2:00	✔	✔	✔	✔	✔	
9:00 to 3:00	✔	✔	✔	✔	✔	✔
10:00 to 4:00	✔					

Count across to tell how many.

Votes for New School Colors

blue and white	✔	✔	✔	✔	✔	
orange and blue	✔	✔				
red and green	✔	✔	✔	✔	✔	✔
yellow and green	✔	✔	✔			

Votes for New Playground Things

swings	✔	✔	✔	✔	✔	
slide	✔	✔				
bat and ball	✔	✔	✔	✔	✔	✔
jump ropes	✔	✔	✔	✔		

Objective: Recognize that charts provide information in a visual format.

**Now find the answers in each group of questions.
Use the charts to help you.**

▼▼▼▼▼▼▼▼▼▼▼▼▼▼▼▼▼▼▼▼▼▼▼▼▼▼▼▼

Votes for New School Hours

1 How many children want to start school at 7:00?

2 Which school hours got only one vote?

3 Which school hours got the most votes?

4 How many children want to end at 4:00?

Votes for New School Colors

5 Which colors got five votes?

6 Which colors got the most votes?

7 How many children voted for orange and blue?

8 How many children voted for yellow and green?

Votes for New Playground Things

9 How many children voted for a bat and ball?

10 Which thing got two votes?

11 Which thing got four votes?

12 How many children voted for the swings?

Answer Box

A three	B red and green	C four	D one	E six	F blue and white
G 10:00 to 4:00	H five	I two	J slide	K jump ropes	L 9:00 to 3:00

Places and Foods We Like

Read each chart.

Count down to tell how many.

Votes for Fun Places to Go

beach	camp	city	farm
✔	✔	✔	✔
✔	✔	✔	✔
✔	✔		✔
✔			✔
			✔

Votes for Favorite Foods for Lunch

salad	chili	milk	apple	cheese	soup
✔	✔	✔	✔	✔	✔
✔	✔	✔	✔	✔	
✔		✔	✔	✔	
✔		✔		✔	
		✔		✔	
				✔	

Objective: Recognize that charts provide information in a visual format.

Now find the answers in each group of questions.
Use the charts to help you.

✪★

Votes for Fun Places to Go

1 How many children like the beach?

2 How many children like the city?

3 What place do the children like best?

4 How many children like to go camping?

5 What do four children like?

6 What do only two children like?

Votes for Favorite Foods for Lunch

7 How many children like cheese?

8 How many children like milk?

9 What food does only one child like?

10 What food do three children like?

11 What food do two children like?

12 What food do five children like?

Answer Box

A	B	C	D	E	F
soup	farm	milk	five	four	three
G	**H**	**I**	**J**	**K**	**L**
chili	beach	two	city	apple	six

Objective: Find information in a chart by reading down columns.

Things We Do

Read the chart.

Things We Did This Week

	Ken	Pam	Li	Jake	Paul	Marla	June	Dina	Alicia
run	✔	✔	✔	✔	✔	✔		✔	✔
climb	✔	✔	✔		✔		✔	✔	✔
skate	✔	✔		✔	✔	✔		✔	✔
swing	✔		✔			✔		✔	
hike		✔	✔	✔	✔	✔	✔	✔	✔
swim		✔		✔				✔	

Objective: Recognize that charts provide information in a visual format.

Now find the answer to each question.
Use the chart to help you.

1 Who did the most things?

2 Who did two things?

3 Who did five things?

4 Who did not hike?

5 How many people did not swim?

6 How many people did six things?

7 How many people marked <u>run</u>?

8 How many people marked <u>climb</u>?

9 How many people marked <u>swim</u>?

10 How many people marked <u>swing</u>?

11 Besides Marla, who did not climb?

12 Besides June, who did not skate?

Think.
Should you
count down
or across?

Answer Box

A	B	C	D	E	F
eight	Dina	one	June	Pam	Jake
G	**H**	**I**	**J**	**K**	**L**
Ken	four	Li	seven	six	three

Objective: Find information in a chart by reading across rows and down columns.

31

Come to My Party!

Read the invitation.

Dear Juan,

Please come to my Halloween party. It will be on October 30 from 3:00 to 6:00. It will be at my house at 20 West Street. Wear a costume. There will be a prize for the best one.

Your friend,

Ana

Now find the answer to each question about the invitation. Use the invitation to help you.

1 It tells about a ▪.

2 It was sent by ▪.

3 It was sent to ▪.

4 The month is ▪.

5 The party will be at ▪.

6 The date of the party is ▪.

7 The party starts at ▪.

8 It ends at ▪.

9 Everyone will wear ▪.

10 The prize is for the ▪.

11 The house is on ▪ Street.

12 The house number is ▪.

Answer Box ···

A	B	C	D	E	F
party	October	costumes	Juan	Ana	October 30
G	**H**	**I**	**J**	**K**	**L**
best costume	3:00	Ana's house	West	6:00	20